SMART STRUCTURES

STADIUMS AND DOMES

Julie Richards

A+

This edition first published in 2004 in the United States of America by
Smart Apple Media.

All rights reserved. No part of this book may be reproduced in any form or by any
means without written permission from the publisher.

Smart Apple Media
1980 Lookout Drive
North Mankato
Minnesota 56003

Library of Congress Cataloging-in-Publication Data
Richards, Julie.
  Stadiums and domes / by Julie Richards.
  p. cm. — (Smart structures)
  Includes index.
  Summary: Describes different kinds of stadiums and domes, the methods and
materials of their construction, and amazing or disastrous examples.
  ISBN 1-58340-349-3
  1. Stadiums—Design and construction—Juvenile literature. 2. Domes—Design
and construction—Juvenile literature. [1. Stadiums—Design and construction.
2. Domes—Design and construction.] I. Title.
  TH4714.R53 2003
  721'.46—dc21

2002044630

First Edition
9 8 7 6 5 4 3 2 1

First published in 2003 by
MACMILLAN EDUCATION AUSTRALIA PTY LTD
627 Chapel Street, South Yarra, Australia 3141

Associated companies and representatives throughout the world.

Copyright © Julie Richards 2003

Edited by Anna Fern
Text design by Cristina Neri, Canary Graphic Design
Cover design by Cristina Neri, Canary Graphic Design
Layout by Nina Sanadze
Illustrations by Margaret Hastie, IKON Computergraphics
Photo research by Legend Images

Printed in Thailand

Acknowledgements
The author and the publisher are grateful to the following for permission to reproduce
copyright material:

Cover photograph: Millennium Dome, London, courtesy of Reuters.

Australian Picture Library/Corbis, pp. 11, 23 (top & bottom), 26; Getty Images, pp. 4,
5 (top left & bottom), 7, 8, 12, 14, 19, 25 (bottom), 29; © 2002 The LEGO Group,
p. 30; Brian Parker, pp. 5 (top right), 9; Photolibrary.com, pp. 16, 21, 25 (top);
Reuters, pp. 1, 18, 20, 27, 28; Sport the Library, p. 24.

While every care has been taken to trace and acknowledge copyright, the publisher
tenders their apologies for any accidental infringement where copyright has proved
untraceable. Where the attempt has been unsuccessful, the publisher welcomes
information that would redress the situation.

CONTENTS

KEY WORDS

When a word is printed in **bold** you can look up its meaning in the key words box on the same page. You can also look up the meaning of words in the glossary on page 31.

STADIUMS AND DOMES AS STRUCTURES

A **structure** is made up of many different parts joined together. The shapes of the parts and the way they are joined together help a structure to stand up and do the job for which it has been designed. The **materials** used to make a structure can be made stronger or weaker, depending on their shape and how they are put together.

Stadiums and **domes** are made by humans. Many stadiums and churches have domed roofs because this is the best way to enclose a large space. For as long as people have wanted to gather together in large groups, they have built domes and stadiums.

Domes and stadiums are built:

- for sporting competitions, exhibitions, and concerts
- as places to honor gods and heroes
- as shelter from extreme temperatures and weather
- to house special equipment, such as telescopes
- to study the environment in a type of laboratory called a biosphere
- as **greenhouses**
- as covers and solar heaters for swimming pools.

▼ Some domes occur in nature. This tortoise has a strong domed shell for protection.

Types of stadiums and domes

There are different types of stadiums and domes made by humans. Many early domes were made of heavy materials that could only be put together in a certain way or the dome would collapse. These domes were usually part of a church and were meant to represent the sky.

Modern domes are made of much lighter materials and have a variety of uses. The type of stadium built by humans depends on how the stadium will be used and how many people will be expected to use it.

The Colosseum, in Rome, Italy, was completed by the ancient Romans in A.D. 80. This stadium was used for entertainment such as gladiator contests and chariot races.

The dome of the Pantheon temple, in Rome, was completed in A.D. 128. This dome was the largest in the world for many hundreds of years. It measures 142 feet (43 m) across and is the same in height.

The Toronto SkyDome, in Canada, is a modern stadium with a dome roof that opens. It was completed in 1989.

An igloo is a domed-shaped house built out of blocks of snow by Inuit people in the Arctic Circle.

LOOKING AT STADIUMS AND DOMES

I f you look very closely at a stadium or dome, you will notice:

- the different parts which have been joined together to build it
- the shapes of these parts.

Stadiums and domes have to carry extremely heavy loads. A stadium must support the weight of the people and the seating inside it. A dome must support itself as part of a roof or other structure. Wind and earthquakes can affect a stadium or a dome by shaking their structure. It is important that the different parts are made into the right shapes and joined together in the right way, or the stadium or dome will not be safe.

Dome shapes

Some shapes are stronger than others. Rectangles, arches, and triangles are the strongest shapes used to build big structures, but they all have their breaking point.

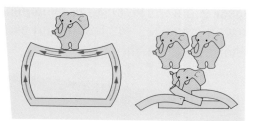

Rectangle

One elephant on a rectangle makes the top side bend. The weight of three elephants causes the top side to break.

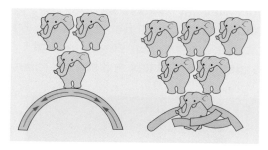

Arch

The weight of three elephants on an arch spreads along the curve to the ground below. The weight of six elephants causes the sides to spread apart and collapse.

Triangle

The weight of six elephants on a triangle causes the two top sides to squeeze together and the bottom side to pull apart. The triangle is the strongest shape, but a herd of elephants makes the bottom side stretch so much that it snaps in half.

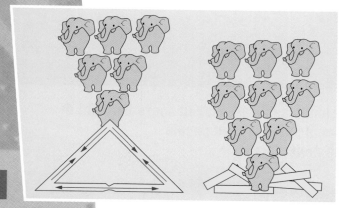

Arches

If you cut a dome in half, you have an arch. An arch is a very strong shape. The ancient Romans discovered that putting arches together made other strong shapes which could be used to cover enormous spaces with only a few columns or pillars for support.

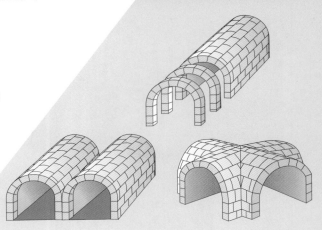

Can weaker shapes be made stronger?

Rectangles are not as strong as triangles. Rectangles can be made stronger by using extra pieces of building material to make them into triangles. An extra piece like this is called a **brace**.

▲ The Romans discovered that if they joined arches together, they could build arched roofs and domes.

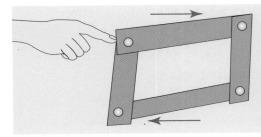 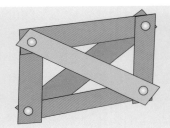 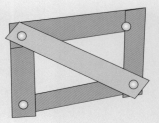

The sides of a rectangle are weak and can be easily moved about.

Fixing two pieces of material to a rectangle makes it stiffer and stronger.

One of the extra pieces can be taken away without weakening the rectangle.

Triangles

Triangles are the strongest, stiffest, and most **stable** of all the shapes.

Triangles can be used to make a round shape such as a dome. In the 1940s, the **architect** Buckminster Fuller made dome structures by **welding** and overlapping many triangles rather than using rows of arches. These geodesic domes, as they are called, are very strong and can be made cheaply from fewer and lighter materials.

Geodesic dome from the 1967 Montreal Expo. Because of its shape, a geodesic dome can cover a large area without the need for roof supports.

THE PARTS OF A STADIUM

Although stadiums might look different, they all have a similar structure. All stadiums have an **arena** and seating which is arranged in stands. Some stadiums have roofs. All of this is supported on a frame, which rests on solid **foundations**.

Seating stands without support columns give spectators a clear view of the action.

Foundations

The foundations of a stadium are like the roots of a tree. They go deep into the ground and stop the stadium from toppling over in the wind or sinking under its own weight.

Foundations are built on solid rock, called bedrock. Bedrock goes deep into Earth's crust. The builders may need to dig deep to find it. Sometimes, the bedrock may be just below the soft surface soil.

Frame

The frame is made up of pieces called members. **Horizontal** members, called beams, support the seating and floors of the stands. **Vertical** members, called columns, support the beams and the roof. The outside walls of the stadium are made from **cladding** materials, which hang on the outside of a frame.

This is a cross-section of a stadium stand. You can see how the stands are angled so that spectators can see all of the arena.

Upper tier of seats

Frame

Middle tier of seats

Lower tier of seats

Stairs

Function rooms

Foundations

Stadium roofs

Stadiums enclose giant spaces, so they have some of the biggest roofs ever built. Some roofs are designed to protect just the spectators from the weather. Others stretch right across the arena, turning the outdoors into indoors. A few stadiums have roofs with sliding sections which can be closed if the weather is bad.

Stadium roofs have to be supported from behind or above to avoid having columns or pillars, which would block the spectators' views. The Minneapolis Metrodome, in Minnesota, has no supports at all! The roof is held in place by steel wires, like a tent. Giant fans blow air into the thin plastic roofing material, keeping it up much like a giant jumping castle.

The roof of the Olympic Park and athletics stadium in Munich, Germany, is made of plastic supported by cables and wires.

Dome roofs

A dome roof can span more than 656 feet (200 m) without any support. The weight of the dome roof goes around the dome walls and down to its rim. The weight would push the rim outwards, so the rim needs to be supported. One way of supporting a dome rim is by using a steel tension ring, which stretches around the dome walls rather like the hoops on a barrel. A tension ring stops the dome walls from pushing outwards and spreading the rim.

When a dome is too heavy, the sides push outwards until cracks appear in the rim at the bottom. A tension ring squeezes the dome and stops the rim from spreading.

BUILDING MATERIALS

The first stadium and dome builders used the natural materials they found around them. Early stadiums and domes were made of heavy stone blocks. The ancient Romans also used **concrete**.

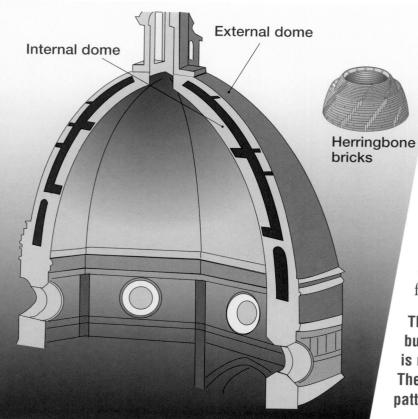

Internal dome

External dome

Herringbone bricks

Ancient Roman **engineers** found ways to make their domes lighter by using pieces of a type of rock called pumice. Pumice contains so many air bubbles that it floats. Using pumice towards the top of a dome made it much lighter.

The first modern domes were made of iron, brick, and concrete. Today, stadiums are made mostly of steel and concrete. Domes can be made of many materials, including plastic, **fiberglass**, and fabric, depending on what they are to be used for and where they are to be built.

The Cathedral of Santa Maria del Fiore was built in Florence, Italy, in the 1400s. Its dome is made from two overlapping brick domes. The bricks have been laid in a herringbone pattern like a woven basket.

Steel

Steel is an **alloy** made mostly of iron. It is used to make the parts of a structure that need to be super-strong. Steel is a much lighter building material than the heavy stone used to build early structures. Steel can also stretch. It is used to make cables, frames, and roof **trusses**. Steel is so strong, a steel cable as thick as your finger could lift a 33-ton (30-t) truck without snapping!

KEY WORDS

concrete a building material made by mixing cement and sand or gravel with water

engineers people who design and build large structures

fiberglass a material made with threads of glass

cathedral the most important Christian church in an area

alloy a mixture of two or more metals

trusses beams made up of a number of pieces welded or bolted together

Concrete

Concrete is a mixture of **cement**, water, sand, and gravel. The wet, runny mixture is poured into molds so that it can be shaped. Concrete dries to become as hard as rock. A mug-sized piece of concrete could support a 33-ton (30-t) truck without crumbling!

Although concrete is very strong when it is squashed, it cracks quite easily when it is stretched. Pouring wet concrete over bunches of steel wires, or a net of steel bars, strengthens the concrete and stops it from cracking as it stretches. This is called **reinforced** concrete. Reinforced concrete is used in the parts of the stadium that will be stretched.

Lighter materials

A stadium roof must be waterproof and strong. It must also be lightweight, because it must be held up by the roof structure. Engineers design roofs made of plastic, fiberglass, and special tough fabrics. It is important that the fabrics do not trap snow, or the roof may collapse. Some roof materials fit over a steel skeleton, while others are held in place by tightly pulled steel cables and wires. Some are clear, to allow natural light into the stadium.

Pier Luigi Nervi showed just how interesting and useful reinforced concrete can be when he built the Florence Stadium in 1930. ▼

KEY WORDS

cement an ingredient in concrete which makes the concrete harden like stone

reinforced made stronger

11

STADIUM DESIGN

All stadiums have a similar structure.

Early stadiums

The ancient Greeks built the first stadiums more than 3,000 years ago for important events such as the Olympic Games. The stadium was longer and thinner than a modern stadium, with a simple track in the arena. Spectators sat on terraces, or steps, which had been carved from natural hillsides. At Olympia, where the Olympic Games were always held, there was enough seating for 30,000 people.

The Colosseum

The Colosseum, in Rome, Italy, is the most famous ancient stadium in the world. The Colosseum is an oval-shaped stadium with an outer wall as high as a 12-story building. The Romans had discovered the strength of the arch and how arches could be joined to make a structure which could enclose a large area without thick supporting pillars. They built the Colosseum as a series of arches joined together to make the oval shape. It had 76 entrances, each with its own stairway leading to a section of seating, and could hold 50,000 people.

Beneath the wooden floor of the arena was a system of tunnels, elevators, trapdoors, and ramps to let the gladiators and wild animals out onto the arena. When a pretend sea battle was staged, the floor of the arena was waterproofed with canvas. Water was piped from the river, flooding the arena deep enough to float full-sized battleships.

◀ **You can see the shape of the Colosseum from this aerial photograph.**

Modern stadiums

Modern stadiums have seating that is arranged like a series of steps so that everyone has a clear view wherever they sit. Although concrete slabs support the seating, it is based on the same idea as the Colosseum and the hillside embankments the ancient Greeks sat on. If you sliced a section of the Colosseum in half, you would see how modern stadium builders have borrowed some of the Roman ideas.

Modern stadium builders are still using some of the same designs first used by ancient engineers. Strong, stable designs will always work, no matter how old they are. ▶

Modern stadiums are often a rounder shape and the arena may be a circle, oval, or rectangle. The seating, the arena shape, and surface can be changed in many modern stadiums so they can be used for a variety of sports and activities.

Modern stadiums are not usually flooded as the Colosseum was, but some have been filled with tons of dirt so that bike shows or BMX competitions can be held.

The main difference between early and modern stadiums is that modern stadiums are usually roofed.

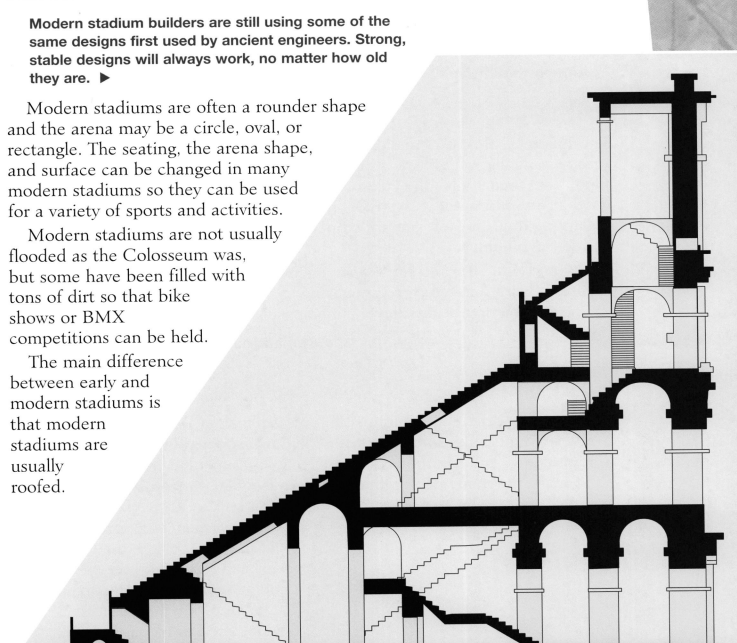

DOME DESIGN

Domes usually form part of the roof of a structure. Most early domes were built on large public structures such as temples, churches, and government buildings.

Early domes

Before domes, almost all ancient buildings were rectangular, with clusters of columns supporting their roofs. The columns were very good at preventing the heavy roofs from collapsing, but they left very little open space inside the building.

Around A.D. 100, ancient Roman engineers realized that a dome was a circular ring of arches. At the top of the dome, curving walls push inward, towards the center, and hold it in a stiff, stable shape.

▲ At the top of this early type of dome, the curving walls push inwards toward the center, making the dome strong and stable.

The Pantheon

The dome of the Pantheon was built by the ancient Romans using bricks and concrete. Like all early domes, the Pantheon was built without any reinforcing. The enormous dome stretches 142 feet (43 m) across. To make the dome lighter, the engineers scooped out some of the concrete in the wall and carved an opening at the top. The sunken panels in the wall show you where the concrete has been removed. Five teenagers could stretch across the opening at the top, which is 27 feet (8 m) wide. The Pantheon remained the world's largest dome for 1,300 years.

◄ The Pantheon, in Rome, Italy

A circular roof over a square room

The Hagia Sofia (Church of the Holy Wisdom), in Constantinople (now Istanbul, in Turkey), was completed in A.D. 537. The architects who designed this building found a way to put a dome over a square space. They rested the edges of the dome on four triangles cut from a circle like pieces of a pie. The rounded edges of the triangles shifted the weight of the dome to the supports below.

Modern domes

Many modern domes are still a part of a roofing structure. Some of the more famous modern domes are Saint Paul's Cathedral, in London, England, and Saint Peter's **Basilica**, in Vatican City, Italy.

Cathedrals

Saint Paul's Cathedral is actually three domes in one. The inside dome was made of bricks and the outside one of wood. Hidden between the two was a brick dome, built in the shape of a cone, which reached up to support the whole structure. This made the dome very strong.

The dome in Saint Peter's Basilica, in Vatican City, has iron chains wrapped around its base. The chains act like a belt to stop the weight of the dome from pressing down and pushing the rim outwards. Later domes replaced the stone with iron ribs, rather like an umbrella frame.

Geodesic domes

Some structures are made up entirely of a dome. Geodesic domes are made from a tight mesh of overlapping triangles. The triangles push against each other and are squeezed with equal force. Geodesic domes come in all sizes. Because of their triangular design, they can be made from a variety of light materials without becoming weak.

Small geodesic domes can be used as greenhouses, storm shelters, and pool domes. Larger geodesic domes can be used as exhibition spaces, theme parks, convention centers, and even indoor botanical gardens.

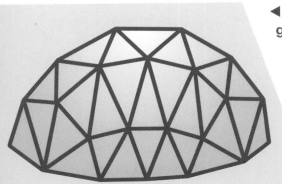

◀ The triangles on a geodesic dome push and squeeze each other with equal force, making the dome very strong.

KEY WORDS

basilica a long, rectangular-shaped church with a rounded wall at one end

Choosing a design

Engineers do a lot of research to make sure they design the right type of stadium or dome. Science has helped engineers to find out about stronger designs, lighter building materials, and new tools that do the job faster. Stadium and dome engineers use many of the shapes that are seen in nature. Shapes such as arches and triangles have proved to be extremely strong, stable shapes for this type of building. A stadium or a dome has to carry a heavy load.

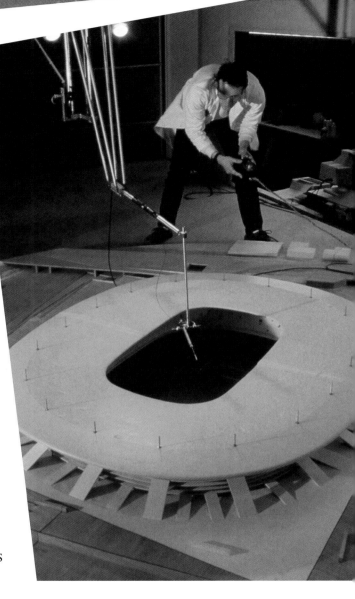

Engineers use a model to show how the stadium will look when it is finished. ▶

Safety and comfort

Architects design all the facilities necessary for the safety and comfort of the spectators. They must consider everything—from the doorways and corridors, to the staircases and escalators—that will allow spectators to reach their seats quickly before an event and to leave again afterwards. Architects also design the cafes, bars, ticket offices, washrooms, and baby-change rooms. Modern stadiums must have facilities for people with special needs. These include wheelchair ramps, special washrooms, and listening devices called hearing loops which allow visually impaired people to listen to a description of what is going on inside the stadium.

A stadium can hold as many people as a small town. A stadium that seats 75,000 spectators needs 800 toilets. All stadiums need services such as electricity, water, gas, and cables for telephones and computers.

BUILDING A STADIUM

Building a large stadium can take hundreds of people several years to finish. Building a stadium in ancient times was an immense challenge. It took eight years to complete the Colosseum.

The Colosseum

Rather than dig deep foundations for the Colosseum, the engineers decided to drain a lake and to pour in a vast oval ring of concrete. The concrete ring was 167 feet (51 m) wide and 39 feet (12 m) deep.

At the same time, stone was being cut for the building blocks. There were no explosives or machines. Every block was cut by hand using a toothless saw. Sand was poured beneath the saw's blade and the stone was gradually worn away. It took nearly 300,000 cartloads of stone to build the Colosseum.

The top part of the structure was made with lighter materials such as wood, light concrete, and bricks. Each arch was built around a wooden frame. Once the arch was finished, the wooden frame was removed. Wooden cranes lifted the stones up to the higher levels where the builders worked on wooden scaffolding which was taken away when the building was finished. The cranes were powered by slaves, walking around and around in a big wheel.

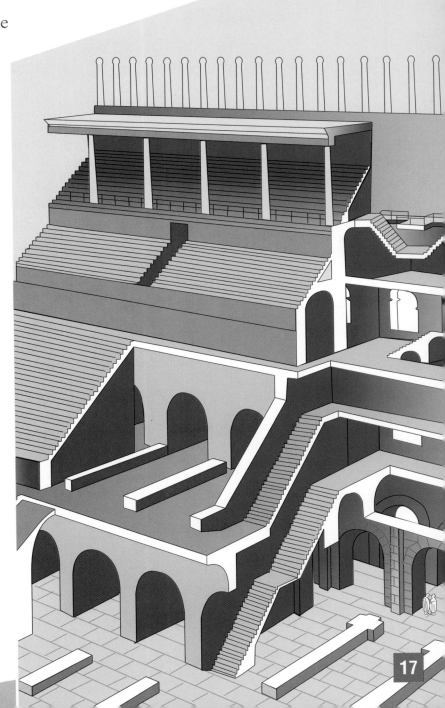

The tiers of seating in the Colosseum are held up by many arches. ▶

Modern stadiums

Building a modern stadium is much easier than it was in the past. Machines do most of the heavy work and building materials are lighter.

Foundations

Digging the foundations of the stadium is the first job to be done. Soft topsoil is dug out by excavating machines and loaded into trucks, to be taken away from the site.

Piles

If the bedrock is just beneath the topsoil, the concrete foundations for the frame are built on top of the rock. If it is deeper down, steel or concrete poles, called piles, will be hammered into the ground by a pile-driver, like nails being knocked into wood. Piles can also be driven in by a drill that spins like a giant corkscrew.

Slab

If the bedrock goes too deep for piles, a concrete slab will be poured over a mesh of steel bars. The reinforced concrete slab acts like a raft, spreading the weight of the stadium over a larger area so that it does not sink into the soft ground. The steel bars are left sticking out of the concrete for the frame to be attached to.

◄ The reinforced concrete slab of a stadium building site

Erecting the frame

The members of the steel frame are made up of flat pieces of steel welded together in a factory. They are brought to the site as they are needed and put together like a giant construction kit using special high-strength nuts and bolts or by welding.

Molding concrete

Some frames are made from concrete. The concrete is delivered to the site and pumped or poured into wooden or metal molds, called formwork. Steel bars are laid inside the formwork and covered with the concrete. Steel bars are left poking out of the columns for the next section to be joined to. Tower cranes are brought to the site and anchored to large concrete blocks or set into a concrete base. They lift the huge pieces of frame or buckets of wet concrete to where they are needed. As the stadium becomes higher, a crane can be made taller by bolting new sections of tower to it. A mobile crane is used to build the first few sections of the tower crane.

The frame of a new stand. Can you see the triangles in the roof support?

The Georgia Dome, in Atlanta, contains enough concrete to build a sidewalk across two states, and 9,296 tons (8,432 t) of steel—more than the weight of iron and steel used in the Eiffel Tower. The Georgia Dome is as tall as a 29-story building. A stadium can be an enormous structure.

Floors and roofs

As the frame of the stadium is erected, work begins on the floors, stairs, and seating slabs. All of these are made from reinforced concrete. The floors are made by laying steel plates side by side, with their ends joined to the beams to make a deck. Concrete is poured onto the deck. The seating slabs, already molded into the right shape, are laid next to each other, or concrete is poured into metal molds containing steel reinforcing bars. Cladding is hung on the outside walls. It might be glass, sheets of metal, or bricks.

A piece of roof is lifted into position by a crane. Temporary supports are used to hold up the roof while the stadium is under construction.

Roofs

When the structure of the stadium is finished, the roof will be added.

Small roofs use trusses stretching from wall to wall to support thin metal or plastic sheets. The weight of the roof is carried by the trusses to the walls and down into the foundations.

In a **cantilever** roof, the beams are connected to the back of the stand and stretch out over the seating.

Some larger roofs are made with thin slabs of reinforced concrete. The strength of concrete roofs comes from their curved or domed shapes, so the concrete may be less than one inch (2 cm) thick at the top of the dome or curve.

There are three ways of supporting a stadium roof. ▼

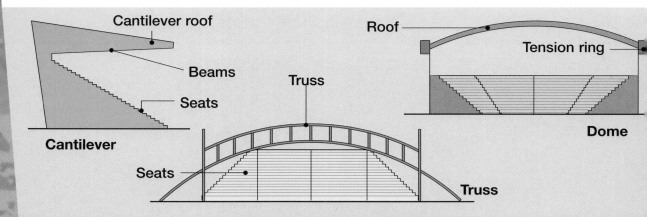

Cantilever roof
Beams
Seats
Cantilever

Truss
Seats
Truss

Roof
Tension ring
Dome

Spectacular roofs

The most spectacular and unusual roofs are those used on giant indoor stadiums.

Hanging by wires

The Georgia Dome has a cable-supported roof 892 feet (272 m) across. The roof is made of a tough, fiberglass fabric which is coated to prevent dirt from sticking to the roof and making it too heavy.

The roof only weighs 68 pounds (30 kg), but it is strong enough to support a truck. How? The roof uses the strength of the triangle. Short, vertical posts carry the weight of the roof. The posts are held in place by stretched steel cables which are connected to the top and bottom of the posts by steel pins and welded joints. The cables pull on the posts like guy ropes on a tent to form strong, tight triangles.

A reinforced concrete ring runs around the dome. The ring rests on a special pad which can slide up and down, allowing the roof material to bend and stretch a little during high winds.

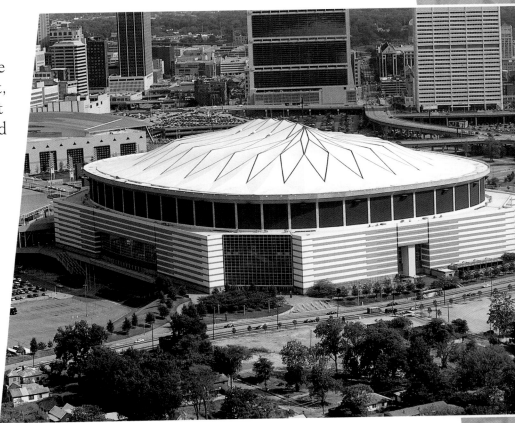

The roof of the Georgia Dome is held up by strong, steel cables which pull on it like guy ropes pull on a tent.

Floating on air

The Pontiac Silverdome, in Michigan, has a fabric roof which is supported by air! The dome is shaped and kept in place by 18 steel cables. The cables are between 600 and 820 feet (183–250 m) long and weigh up to 15,000 pounds (6,800 kg) each. They were installed by a giant Sikorsky Skycrane helicopter. A concrete-and-steel ring around the rim of the dome anchors the cables and stops the rim from spreading outwards. Air is forced up into the dome by 25 fans. The stadium has 50 revolving entrance doors which stop the air from rushing out. An alarm sounds if there is not enough air to keep the dome up.

Retractable roofs

A roof that opens by sliding back into itself, like a tortoise going into its shell, is called a retractable roof. On a sunny day, the SkyDome stadium in Toronto, Canada, separates into pieces and disappears from sight in less than 20 minutes. How does it do this? The roof has four massive steel panels. One panel is fixed, while the other three moveable panels sit on steel tracks. When the roof opens, two of the moving panels slide over each other and under the fixed panel. The third panel slides on a circular track until it, too, is beneath the fixed panel. The whole roof weighs more than 12,321 tons (11,176 t), yet the panels slide at 71 feet (21.6 m) per minute.

The SkyDome, in Toronto, Canada ▼

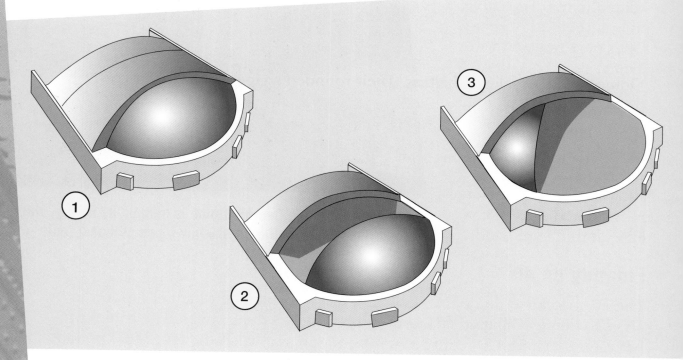

The roof covers a massive area. In 1992, the SkyDome set the world record for the greatest number of hot-air balloons in an enclosed space—46 fully inflated balloons on the playing field! Eight Boeing 747s could fit on the field. Even with the roof closed, a 31-story building or the Colosseum could fit inside the SkyDome.

Domes

Not all domes are on roofs. Some domes can be a structure by themselves.

Geodesic domes

Geodesic domes have many uses. The Climatron, in Missouri, is a giant greenhouse in the Missouri Botanical Garden. The dome has a diameter of 190 feet (58 m) and was originally built using an aluminum frame with see-through plastic panes. When the plastic panes needed replacing with heavier glass panes, engineers realized that the aluminum frame would not be strong enough to support them. The engineers decided to build a dome within a dome— a bit like Saint Paul's Cathedral in London. They built a second dome of aluminum pipes and connected it by rods to the old frame from the inside. The inner dome supports the outer dome with its heavy glass panes. The Climatron now contains 3,625 panes of glass. The way the panes of glass lie makes 72 different and interesting triangular shapes.

The Climatron is a dome within a dome. Can you see the different triangular shapes?

Small domes

Domes make excellent shelters. Their rounded shape means fewer costly building materials are needed, they use less energy for heating, and their smooth shape makes them wind resistant.

The domes used by Antarctic scientists are called apples. Their bright-red color is easily seen against the snow. Domes are also useful as emergency shelters. Being made of very light material means they can be dropped into a disaster area by helicopter.

This dome-shaped home saves energy and offers good protection against storms. Dome homes can be built quickly, easily, and cheaply.

WORKING STADIUMS AND DOMES

Once a stadium is finished and services such as electricity, gas, telephones, and water are installed, it is prepared for use. The surface is laid and safety fences are added. A grass surface is often planted in trays the same shape as a honeycomb made by bees. This is a very good shape because it uses all the available space very **efficiently**. Some playing surfaces are made of **synthetic** materials, which need very little looking after compared with real grass. As well as lighting for the spectators, electronic video scoreboards made of many thousands of lightbulbs are added. The SkyDome's scoreboard has 420,000 lightbulbs, making it the largest scoreboard in the world.

Changing the stadium around

A few stadiums can be used for more than one purpose. These stadiums have an arena that can change its shape or size, depending on the event. The front rows of seats are movable and can be set up as a temporary stand closer to the action or, if they are not needed, hidden away beneath the lower part of the stand.

▲ Here the Vodafone Arena, in Australia, is being used as a tennis court.

▲ Here the Vodafone Arena is being used for a cycling race.

A synthetic playing surface can also be temporarily removed. Synthetic surfaces are usually wound around huge rollers and stored in a pit beneath the stadium floor. Some are on a series of decks which are brought out from under the stands and fixed into place.

At the Pontiac Silverdome, jets of air are used to float the playing surface over the stadium floor. It takes 30 minutes for a crew of 10 people to properly install the playing surface.

KEY WORDS

efficiently doing something without waste
synthetic made by humans

24

Biospheres

Scientists sometimes study the environment by building a biosphere. A biosphere is like a mini-Earth inside a geodesic dome or series of domes. A biosphere can have its own desert, jungle, and even an indoor sea with a coral reef. The climate inside a biosphere is carefully controlled to suit each type of environment. People can live inside a biosphere.

▲ **The Eden Project**

Biospheres help scientists to work out how to build shelters with controlled environments that will allow humans to live in space or deep under the ocean.

Not all biospheres are designed for experiments. The Eden Project, in England, is a biosphere exhibition that highlights the need for people to have a better relationship with the environment. Visitors to the Eden Project can experience Earth's different environments without having to travel far.

Observatories

An observatory is a place with a domed roof where giant telescopes are kept. When a telescope is used, a section of the roof opens and slides back over itself, giving the telescope an uninterrupted view of the night sky. The rim of the dome has wheels or a special track inside it. When a motor is switched on, the dome can be turned to face in any direction.

Part of this observatory slides open so that the night sky can be viewed. ▶

Solar domes

Smaller solar domes trap lots of sunlight and get very warm. People use them to heat the area around an outdoor swimming pool, as a place to sit when the weather is cooler, and as a greenhouse.

Looking after stadiums and domes

A stadium needs to be kept clean, tidy, and in good repair. Teams of cleaners clean up after each event and clear away garbage. Other workers make sure that the telephones, electricity, and water supplies are always working. The special materials on the stadium playing surface need to be looked after. If the surface is grass, gardeners water and feed the grass and replace any grass that dies. If the stadium has a retractable domed roof, the motors and wheels must be kept running smoothly.

STADIUMS AND DOMES THAT WENT WRONG

The roofs and stands of modern stadiums are designed to stand up to earthquakes, heavy snow, and high winds. But if there is a problem with a stadium's structure, it may not be known until a terrible accident occurs. Not all engineers have enough knowledge about making structures strong and stable. Sometimes, not enough money is spent on the right materials.

Collapses and fires

A large crowd of excited people packed together in a stadium can turn into a very dangerous situation should there be an emergency. In 1985, at the Bradford City Football Club, in England, 56 people died when piles of garbage beneath an old wooden stand caught fire. Fire swept through in five minutes, trapping the victims. Afterwards, fire regulations were improved at other grounds.

In 1992, in the French town of Bastia, 15 spectators died and 2,000 were injured when a temporary stand, built from metal scaffolding, collapsed before a soccer match.

▲ The stand collapse at Bastia, France.
You can see how important it is for engineers to get it right.

Crowd disasters

Some older stadiums have places without seats where people can stand and watch. This makes it possible for a stadium to become dangerously overcrowded because lots of extra people can be squeezed in. In 1989, at the Hillsborough soccer stadium, in England, fans arriving just as the match started pushed into the stadium, crushing people in front against a security fence. Ninety-six people were killed and 200 were injured. Standing areas and security fences have since been banned.

Problem domes

Some domes and stadiums have experienced problems during building.

Montreal

When Canada hosted the 1976 Olympic Games, the Montreal Olympic stadium was not finished. It was one of the first stadiums to be capped with a plastic roof, but problems arose when it was discovered that a tower that was part of the retractable roof system would be too heavy if built in concrete. The stadium was eventually completed in 1987.

The tower was built from steel and the roof was made from a synthetic fabric called Kevlar—the same material used in bullet-proof vests. Attached to 26 steel cables, the enormous roof was supposed to fold into the tower like a giant umbrella. It never did.

In 1991, there was another mishap when a 62-ton (56-t) concrete beam crashed onto a walkway. Luckily, nobody was hurt, but the stadium had to be closed for several weeks. By 1998, the stadium had a new, non-retractable roof.

The old Kevlar roof of the Montreal stadium being removed ▼

AMAZING STADIUMS AND DOMES

Many of the world's most amazing structures are stadiums and domes. Some are record-breakers because of their size or their design. Others broke records because they were the first to use certain building materials or because ways of solving difficult problems were found during their building. Here are some interesting facts and figures, but there are many more you can find out about.

The Millennium Dome

The Millennium Dome, in London, England, is not a true dome. This is because its fabric roof is really supported by a web of 2,600 steel cables suspended from a circle of 12 gigantic steel masts. The design is similar to a spider's web. The masts were so long and so heavy that one of the largest cranes in Europe was needed to raise them into position. The crane was so huge, it took 24 trucks to bring all of its sections to the dome site.

Resting on 8,000 piles that go 78 feet (24 m) into the ground, the Millennium Dome is 165 feet (50 m) high—as high as Nelson's Column and the Statue of Liberty (without its base). It is 984 feet (300 m) wide—enough room for the Eiffel Tower lying on its side!

The Millennium Dome is not a real dome because its roof is supported by cables attached to masts.

Stadium firsts

- The biggest stadium ever built was the Circus Maximus, in ancient Rome. It held 250,000 spectators.
- The Colosseum was the first stadium to have its seats in tiers.
- The Astrodome, in Houston, Texas, was the first large indoor stadium. It was built in 1966.

Stadiums and dome facts

A popular synthetic playing surface called Astroturf was invented at the Astrodome in Houston. The Astrodome's roof contained 4,007 skylights to let the light in. Unfortunately, the skylights turned the sun's rays into a blinding wall of light, making it impossible to see a ball in the air. The skylights were painted to block the sun, but the grass died from lack of sunlight. Plastic grass was installed and it became known as "Astroturf."

Stadium world records

Largest *capacity*
Maracana Stadium, Rio de Janeiro, Brazil. This stadium can hold 150,000 spectators. It would take that many people two-and-a-half days to walk through a single entrance!

Tallest floodlight towers
Melbourne Cricket Ground, Australia. The towers are 246 feet (75 m) high.

KEY WORDS

capacity the maximum amount something can hold

Largest roof area
Munich Olympic Stadium, Germany. The roof covers the same area as 17 soccer fields.

This is the immense bowl of the Maracana Stadium, Rio de Janeiro, Brazil. ▶

Stadium trivia

- The 44,100 tons (40,000 t) of concrete used in the Millennium Stadium built in 1999, in Wales, would have taken about 30 years to mix by hand!
- The word "stadium" comes from an Ancient Greek measurement called a *stade* (about 623 feet or 190 m), which was the length of a race. A stadium was a place where people watched a *stade* race.

USING MODELS TO LEARN ABOUT STRUCTURES

You can find out about some of the challenges engineers meet when they design and build a stadium or a dome by using a construction set to build your own. Construction sets have the same parts as stadiums and domes. They have pieces that can be joined or screwed together to make a framework, bases that act as foundations, and roof supports, too.

Strength and stability are just as important in a construction set as they are in a life-sized structure. Many of today's engineers and architects started with construction sets. They are still building with them—the construction sets just grew bigger.

▲ Construction sets are a great way to learn about strong and stable domes and stadiums.

alloy	a mixture of two or more metals
architect	a person who designs buildings
arena	a center space where contests and sports take place
basilica	a long, rectangular-shaped church with a rounded wall at one end
brace	something fastened to an object to keep it stiff and straight, just like the braces worn on teeth
cantilever	a beam fixed at one end and supporting a structure at the other
capacity	the maximum amount something can hold
cathedral	the most important Christian church in an area
cement	an ingredient in concrete which makes the concrete harden like stone
cladding	covering
concrete	a building material made by mixing cement and sand or gravel with water
domes	round roofs
efficiently	doing something without waste
engineers	people who design and build large structures
fiberglass	a material made with threads of glass
foundations	a firm base upon which a structure is built
greenhouses	glass buildings where plants that need to be kept warm are grown
horizontal	level or flat
materials	anything used to make a structure
reinforced	made stronger
stable	something that will not wobble or fall
structure	something that is made up of many parts joined together
synthetic	made by humans
trusses	beams made up of a number of pieces welded or bolted together
vertical	standing upright
welding	joining pieces of metal together by heating their edges until they melt into one

INDEX